AF668789

Olympiad ACE

A Comprehensive Practice Book

for School Olympiads & Talent Search Exams

SOCIAL STUDIES

Class 3

BLOOM
Founded by | arihant

Olympiad ACE

A Comprehensive Practice Book

for School Olympiads & Talent Search Exams

SOCIAL STUDIES

Class 3

by

Adhishree Neurgaonkar

Olympiad ACE

Bloom Cap Edu Ventures Pvt. Ltd.

卐 **Administrative & Production Office**
'Ramchhaya' 4577/15, Agarwal Road, Darya Ganj, New Delhi -110002
Tele: 011- 47630600, 43518550

卐 **PRICE:** ₹125.00

卐 PO No. : TXT-59-T064515-04-25

Published by Arihant Publications (I) Ltd.

For further information about the books log on to
www.bloomcap.org

Follow us on

Preface

"Future belongs to those Who prepares for it today"

School Olympiads are National & International level competitions conducted by different Government, Non-Government & Educational Organisations with the purpose of making the children ready to face competitive exams.

The challenging Questions asked in Olympiads motivate them to learn more & more and bring out the best results with improved academic performance. The Awards & Scholarship offered by Olympiads motivate children to aspire & strive for doing better and emerge out to be the best.

Social Studies Olympiads

Social Studies provides students with a comprehensive understanding of society, politics, economics and history. Studying Social Studies helps students understand the complexities of society, and prepares them for careers in fields such as public service, education, law, journalism, and research.

Social Studies Olympiads are meant to develop students' interest towards this vital subject.

'Bloom Social Studies Olympiad Study Book Class 3' is a perfect resource to Study & Practice for Olympiad Exams and other National & State Level Talent Search Exams & Other Competitions.

Some Special Features of Bloom Social Studies Olympiad Study Books are;

- Complete coverage of all the aspects of History, Geography and Civics.
- Chapterwise Exercises having different types of Objective Questions at par with the Olympiad Level.
- Olympiad Pattern Practice Sets at the end.

This book is prepared by Expert Panel with the utmost care, still if you have any suggestions regarding its improvement then feel free to contact us at support@bloomcap.org. We will try to inculcate your suggestions in the further editions.

Contents

01

The Earth and the Solar System

MCQs 1 Mark Questions

1. What is the collection of stars and planets called?
(a) Galaxy (b) Asteroid
(c) Meteoroid (d) Comet

2. Which of the following planets is known as 'Morning Star' or 'Evening Star'?
(a) Mercury (b) Venus
(c) Mars (d) Earth

3. Identify the planet of Solar System which is not visible to the naked eyes.
(a) Saturn (b) Jupiter
(c) Neptune (d) Venus

4. When a group or cluster of stars form a definite pattern, it is known as ....
(a) Constellation (b) Galaxy
(c) Meteoroid (d) Asteroid

5. Which of the following is the brightest planet of the Solar System?
(a) Earth (b) Mercury
(c) Jupiter (d) Venus

6. What are the small planetary bodies seen mostly between the orbits of Mars and Jupiter called?
(a) Asteroids (b) Comets
(c) Galaxy (d) Meteoroids

7. Complete the given analogy.
Blue Planet : Earth : : ? : Mars
(a) Red Planet (b) Green Planet
(c) White Planet (d) Brown Planet

8. The layer of air around the Earth is known as ....

(a) Hydrosphere (b) Atmosphere

(c) Lithosphere (d) Biosphere

9. Identify the effect of revolution of the Earth from the given options.

(a) It causes longer days and shorter nights.

(b) It causes different seasons.

(c) It causes day and night.

(d) None of the above

10. What is the term used for spinning of the Earth on its own axis ?

(a) Revolution (b) Rotation

(c) Movement (d) Orbiting

11. The sailors went around the world starting from one point and then coming back to that same point. What could be the possible reason behind this phenomenon?

(a) The Earth is spherical in shape.

(b) The Earth is flat.

(c) The shape of the Earth is oval.

(d) The shape of the Earth is round.

12. Choose the odd one out.

(a) Atmosphere (b) Lithosphere

(c) Galaxy (d) Hydrosphere

13. Which layer of the Earth is made up of rocks and provides us with minerals?

(a) Lithosphere

(b) Hydrosphere

(c) Biosphere

(d) Atmosphere

14. The Earth is divided into two equal parts that are Northern hemisphere and Southern hemisphere by an imaginary line. Identify this imaginary line.

(a) Tropic of Capricorn (b) Equator

(c) North Pole (d) Tropic of Cancer

15. How much percentage of the Earth, is covered with water?

(a) 60% (b) 71%

(c) 85% (d) 75%

16. **Identify the landform represented by the given picture.**

(a) Mountain (b) Valley
(c) Plateau (d) Plain

17. **Complete the given analogy.**

Largest Continent : Asia :: Smallest Continent : ?

(a) Europe (b) Australia
(c) North America (d) Africa

18. **What are the total number of continents present on the surface of the Earth?**

(a) Five (b) Six
(c) Seven (d) Eight

19. **......... is the curved path followed by a planet as it moves around the Sun.**

(a) Great Circle
(b) Orbit
(c) Equator
(d) Both (a) and (b)

20. **Which instrument is shown in the picture given below?**

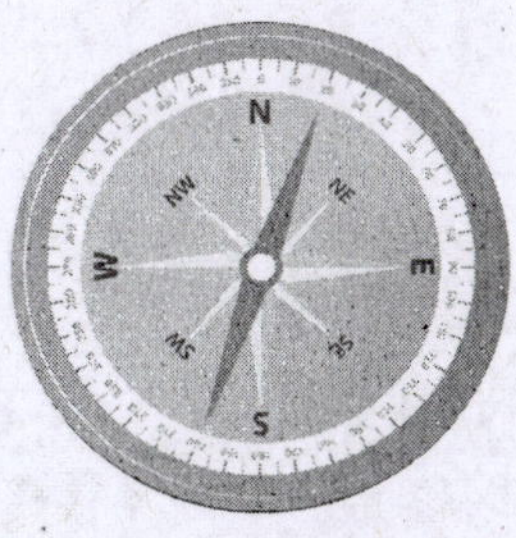

(a) Globe (b) Map
(c) Compass (d) Atlas

21. Choose the incorrect statement.

(a) The needle of compass always points towards the North.
(b) Sailors use the compass for navigation.
(c) Compass shows two major directions only *i.e.,* North and South.
(d) None of the above

22. Unscramble the letters given in the options to obtain the name of the continent which is also called as Dark Continent.

(a) RIFACA (b) SAIA
(c) RUOEPE (d) None of these

23. Identify the following.

I. I am the smallest ocean in the world.
II. I am the only ocean named after a country.

Choose the correct option.

	I	II
(a)	Indian	Pacific
(b)	Pacific	Atlantic
(c)	Antarctic	Indian
(d)	Arctic	Indian

24. Read the following statements and select which ones are true (T) and which ones are false (F).

I. Atmosphere is a mixture of important gases such as nitrogen, oxygen and carbon dioxide.
II. Neptune is the coldest planet of the Solar System.

Codes

	I	II
(a)	T	F
(b)	F	T
(c)	T	T
(d)	F	F

25. **Match the following.**

List I	List II
A. Twin Planet of the Earth	1. Mercury
B. Closest Planet	2. Venus
C. Farthest Planet	3. Saturn
D. Ringed Planet	4. Neptune

Codes

	A	B	C	D		A	B	C	D
(a)	2	1	4	3	(b)	4	3	1	2
(c)	1	2	3	4	(d)	3	1	2	4

26. **Identify the following.**

I. I am a heavenly body that moves around the Sun.

II. I am a vehicle that travels to space.

Choose the correct option.

	I	II		I	II
(a)	Planet	Spacecraft	(b)	Galaxy	Planet
(c)	Spacecraft	Planet	(d)	Planet	Galaxy

27. **Read the given statements carefully.**

I. They are large water bodies, usually with land on several sides.

II. They have salty water.

Which water body are we talking about?

(a) Lakes (b) Rivers

(c) Oceans (d) Seas

Darken your choice with HB Pencil

1.	ⓐ ⓑ ⓒ ⓓ	6.	ⓐ ⓑ ⓒ ⓓ	11.	ⓐ ⓑ ⓒ ⓓ	16.	ⓐ ⓑ ⓒ ⓓ	21.	ⓐ ⓑ ⓒ ⓓ	26.	ⓐ ⓑ ⓒ ⓓ
2.	ⓐ ⓑ ⓒ ⓓ	7.	ⓐ ⓑ ⓒ ⓓ	12.	ⓐ ⓑ ⓒ ⓓ	17.	ⓐ ⓑ ⓒ ⓓ	22.	ⓐ ⓑ ⓒ ⓓ	27.	ⓐ ⓑ ⓒ ⓓ
3.	ⓐ ⓑ ⓒ ⓓ	8.	ⓐ ⓑ ⓒ ⓓ	13.	ⓐ ⓑ ⓒ ⓓ	18.	ⓐ ⓑ ⓒ ⓓ	23.	ⓐ ⓑ ⓒ ⓓ		
4.	ⓐ ⓑ ⓒ ⓓ	9.	ⓐ ⓑ ⓒ ⓓ	14.	ⓐ ⓑ ⓒ ⓓ	19.	ⓐ ⓑ ⓒ ⓓ	24.	ⓐ ⓑ ⓒ ⓓ		
5.	ⓐ ⓑ ⓒ ⓓ	10.	ⓐ ⓑ ⓒ ⓓ	15.	ⓐ ⓑ ⓒ ⓓ	20.	ⓐ ⓑ ⓒ ⓓ	25.	ⓐ ⓑ ⓒ ⓓ		

02

Four Different Seasons

MCQs 1 Mark Questions

1. Which is the only natural satellite of the Earth?

(a) Sun (b) Moon
(c) Star (d) Comet

2. The Earth takes 365 days and 6 hours to complete one revolution. What is this time period called?

(a) Solar year (b) Leap year
(c) Current year (d) None of these

3. The annual motion of the Earth is also known as .... of the Earth.

(a) rotation (b) encircling
(c) orbiting (d) revolution

4. The changes in the length of day and night is caused by which of the following phenomena?

(a) Rotation (b) Revolution
(c) Variation (d) Movement

5. When there is summer in Northern hemisphere, the Southern hemisphere experiences ....

(a) winter (b) autumn
(c) summer (d) spring

6. How many seasons does the world experience?

(a) Six (b) Three
(c) Four (d) Five

7. In which of the following seasons the length of day and night is equal?

(a) Summer (b) Winter
(c) Autumn (d) Rainy

8. What is the duration of days and nights in summer?

(a) Short days and long nights
(b) Equal days and equal nights
(c) Short days and short nights
(d) Long days and short nights

9. Which part of India have hot summers and very cold winters?

(a) Northern (b) Southern
(c) Eastern (d) Western

10. What is the correct order of the seasons?

(a) Spring, Summer, Autumn, Winter
(b) Summer, Spring, Winter, Autumn
(c) Winter, Summer, Autumn, Spring
(d) Spring, Summer, Winter, Autumn

11. In this season, the weather is same as that of spring, but trees shed leaves and look barren. Identify the season.

(a) Winter (b) Summer
(c) Autumn (d) Monsoon

12. Which season is also known as harvest season in several regions of the world?

(a) Spring (b) Summer
(c) Autumn (d) Rainy

13. During winters, the .... are longer than the ....

(a) nights, days
(b) days, nights
(c) Both (a) and (b)
(d) None of the above

14. Why the people in Australia celebrates Christmas in summers?

(a) Australia lies in Northern hemisphere.
(b) Australia lies near equator.
(c) Australia lies in Southern hemisphere.
(d) None of the above

15. Identify the season which is an ideal time for practicing the sport shown in the picture given below.

(a) Summer (b) Autumn
(c) Winter (d) Spring

16. Which of the following is not a reason for the existence of seasons?

(a) The movement of the Sun.
(b) The tilt of the Earth on its axis.
(c) The rotation of the Earth on its axis.
(d) The Earth's orbit around the Sun.

17. Monsoons are the .... winds that brings rain to India.

(a) dry (b) hot
(c) seasonal (d) cold

18. Complete the given analogy.

Mawsynram : Meghalaya : : Thar Desert : ?

(a) Gujarat (b) Rajasthan
(c) Maharashtra (d) Madhya Pradesh

19. Choose the correct statement from the following.

(a) Synthetic clothes are preferred in winters.
(b) Cotton clothes are preferred in regions with heavy snowfall.
(c) Dark colour clothes are preferred in summers.
(d) None of the above

20. Match the following.

List I	List II
A. Christmas is celebrated	1. Winter
B. Seasonal winds	2. Spring
C. Trees shed their leaves	3. Monsoon
D. New leaves on trees	4. Autumn

Codes

	A	B	C	D		A	B	C	D
(a)	1	3	4	2	(b)	1	2	3	4
(c)	4	3	2	1	(d)	4	2	3	1

21. Read the following statements carefully and answer the following question.

I. Houses are built with sloping roofs.

II. There is heavy snowfall.

Which season are we talking about?

(a) Summer (b) Winter (c) Spring (d) Monsoon

22. Read the following statements and select which ones are true (T) and which ones are false (F).

I. Houses are built according to the climate of a place.

II. The Northern hemisphere is located to the East of equator.

Codes

	I	II		I	II
(a)	T	T	(b)	F	T
(c)	T	F	(d)	F	F

23. Unscramble the letters given in the options to form the name of a season which is experienced in June and September months.

(a) MMSURE (b) AIRYN

(c) PISRGN (d) TUAMUN

Darken your choice with HB Pencil

1.	ⓐ ⓑ ⓒ ⓓ	5.	ⓐ ⓑ ⓒ ⓓ	9.	ⓐ ⓑ ⓒ ⓓ	13.	ⓐ ⓑ ⓒ ⓓ	17.	ⓐ ⓑ ⓒ ⓓ	21.	ⓐ ⓑ ⓒ ⓓ
2.	ⓐ ⓑ ⓒ ⓓ	6.	ⓐ ⓑ ⓒ ⓓ	10.	ⓐ ⓑ ⓒ ⓓ	14.	ⓐ ⓑ ⓒ ⓓ	18.	ⓐ ⓑ ⓒ ⓓ	22.	ⓐ ⓑ ⓒ ⓓ
3.	ⓐ ⓑ ⓒ ⓓ	7.	ⓐ ⓑ ⓒ ⓓ	11.	ⓐ ⓑ ⓒ ⓓ	15.	ⓐ ⓑ ⓒ ⓓ	19.	ⓐ ⓑ ⓒ ⓓ	23.	ⓐ ⓑ ⓒ ⓓ
4.	ⓐ ⓑ ⓒ ⓓ	8.	ⓐ ⓑ ⓒ ⓓ	12.	ⓐ ⓑ ⓒ ⓓ	16.	ⓐ ⓑ ⓒ ⓓ	20.	ⓐ ⓑ ⓒ ⓓ		

03

Environment and Water Around us

MCQs 1 Mark Questions

1. The Earth is surrounded by a blanket of air. What is it called?
(a) Atmosphere
(b) Hydrosphere
(c) Biosphere
(d) Lithosphere

2. The Earth's atmosphere is made up of different gases. Which of the following gases is/are present in the air?
(a) Nitrogen
(b) Oxygen
(c) Carbon dioxide
(d) All of these

3. Plants take in .... and give out ....
(a) oxygen, carbon dioxide
(b) carbon dioxide, oxygen
(c) oxygen, hydrogen
(d) carbon dioxide, nitrogen

4. Identify which among the following gases is used by plants to make their food.
(a) Oxygen
(b) Carbon dioxide
(c) Nitrogen
(d) Hydrogen

5. What would happen if there is no air?
(a) There would be no plants.
(b) There would be no life.
(c) There would be no animals.
(d) All of the above

6. Which type of energy can be generated by the structure shown in the picture given below?

(a) Solar energy (b) Wind energy
(c) Hydel energy (d) None of these

7. Water is the main constituent of the Earth. Identify how much portion of the Earth is covered with water.

(a) Three-fourth (b) One-third
(c) Two-third (d) Half

8. Which among the following is/are the natural source(s) of water?

(a) Rivers (b) Lakes
(c) Seas (d) All of these

9. Choose the odd one out.

(a) Lakes (b) Dams
(c) Tube wells (d) Canals

10. Which of the following sources of water is used by companies to produce electricity on a large scale?

(a)  (b) 

(c)  (d) 

11. **The drops of water that fall from the clouds in the sky is known as ....**

(a) fog (b) rain (c) ice (d) water vapour

12. **Complete the given analogy.**

Ice : Solid : : ? : Liquid

(a) Nitrogen (b) Mercury (c) Copper (d) Both (a) and (b)

13. **Choose the correct statement(s) regarding evaporation.**

(a) Changing of solid into liquid (b) Changing of liquid into gas

(c) Changing of gas into liquid (d) Both (a) and (b)

14. **Which among the following is/are the main constituent(s) of our environment?**

(a) Air (b) Water

(c) Soil (d) All of these

15. **Environmental pollution is the main cause of concern today. What is/are the main cause(s) of it?**

(a) Afforestation (b) Industrialisation

(c) Deforestation (d) Both (b) and (c)

16. **Which of the following is/are the human made sources of water?**

(a) Dams (b) Tube wells

(c) Canals (d) All of these

17. **When the harmful substances are released into the water bodies, it is called ....**

(a) soil pollution (b) noise pollution

(c) water pollution (d) air pollution

18. **Air pollution is a major problem in cities. Identify the harmful gases which causes air pollution.**

(a) Nitrogen (b) Oxygen

(c) Carbon dioxide (d) Hydrogen

19. **Rita lives in city where there is a lot of noise from traffic, horns and firecrackers. In this case, what will be the harmful effect of noise on her health?**

(a) Loss of hearing (b) Cold and cough

(c) Breathing problem (d) None of these

20. Which of the following is the top layer of the Earth in which plants and trees grows?

(a) Soil (b) Ozone
(c) Mantle (d) Core

21. What is the harmful effect of the kind of pollution shown in the picture given below?

(a) Lack of potable water (b) Problem in breathing
(c) Hearing problem (d) None of these

22. How many objects given in the box are solid in state?

Oxygen, Table, Juice, Pencil, Water, Oil, Chair, Computer, Milk, Toy

(a) Four (b) Six
(c) Five (d) Three

23. Identify the incorrect statement from the options given below.

I. Air is a mixture of many gases and gaseous substances.
II. Slow moving air is called wind.

Codes
(a) Only I
(b) Only II
(c) Both I and II
(d) Neither I nor II

24. Unscramble the letters given in the options to find the name of a lake with the help of information given below.

(a) SAPCAIN (b) PEUSIROR
(c) BLRAET (d) None of these

25. Match the following.

List I	List II
A. Cloud	1. Frozen form of water
B. Water vapour	2. Moving air
C. Ice	3. Gaseous state of water when water boils
D. Wind	4. A white or grey mass of very small droplets of water that floats in sky

Codes

	A	B	C	D		A	B	C	D
(a)	4	3	1	2	(b)	3	1	2	4
(c)	1	3	4	2	(d)	2	3	4	1

26. Read the following statements and select which ones are true (T) and which ones are false (F).

I. Water that is safe to drink is called potable water.

II. The process of changing of water from one form to other is called water cycle.

Codes

	I	II		I	II
(a)	F	F	(b)	F	T
(c)	T	F	(d)	T	T

Darken your choice with HB Pencil

1.	ⓐ ⓑ ⓒ ⓓ	6.	ⓐ ⓑ ⓒ ⓓ	11.	ⓐ ⓑ ⓒ ⓓ	16.	ⓐ ⓑ ⓒ ⓓ	21.	ⓐ ⓑ ⓒ ⓓ	26.	ⓐ ⓑ ⓒ ⓓ
2.	ⓐ ⓑ ⓒ ⓓ	7.	ⓐ ⓑ ⓒ ⓓ	12.	ⓐ ⓑ ⓒ ⓓ	17.	ⓐ ⓑ ⓒ ⓓ	22.	ⓐ ⓑ ⓒ ⓓ		
3.	ⓐ ⓑ ⓒ ⓓ	8.	ⓐ ⓑ ⓒ ⓓ	13.	ⓐ ⓑ ⓒ ⓓ	18.	ⓐ ⓑ ⓒ ⓓ	23.	ⓐ ⓑ ⓒ ⓓ		
4.	ⓐ ⓑ ⓒ ⓓ	9.	ⓐ ⓑ ⓒ ⓓ	14.	ⓐ ⓑ ⓒ ⓓ	19.	ⓐ ⓑ ⓒ ⓓ	24.	ⓐ ⓑ ⓒ ⓓ		
5.	ⓐ ⓑ ⓒ ⓓ	10.	ⓐ ⓑ ⓒ ⓓ	15.	ⓐ ⓑ ⓒ ⓓ	20.	ⓐ ⓑ ⓒ ⓓ	25.	ⓐ ⓑ ⓒ ⓓ		

04

The Early Human Beings

MCQs 1 Mark Questions

1. **Why early humans called as hunters and gatherers?**
   (a) They get their food from animals.
   (b) They get their food from plants.
   (c) Both (a) and (b)
   (d) They gather resources from the forest for their food and shelter.

2. **Since the early man moved from place to place, they were known as ....**
   (a) hunters
   (b) gatherers
   (c) nomads
   (d) farmers

3. **Due to which of the following reasons, the early man started living in caves?**
   (a) To protect themselves from weather.
   (b) To protect themselves from wild animals.
   (c) To grow food.
   (d) All of the above

4. **The early humans didn't have woollen clothes to protect themselves from severe cold. How did they covered their body to protect themselves from cold?**
   (a) Grass
   (b) Animal skin
   (c) Leaves and bark of trees
   (d) All of the above

5. **In early stages, what were the qualities of man?**
   (a) Polite and civilised
   (b) Rough and polite
   (c) Civilised and tough
   (d) Rough and uncivilised

6. **Which of the following materials is/are used by the early man to make tools and weapons?**

(a) Wood (b) Stones
(c) Leaves (d) Both (a) and (b)

7. **Identify the picture given below and mark the correct answer.**

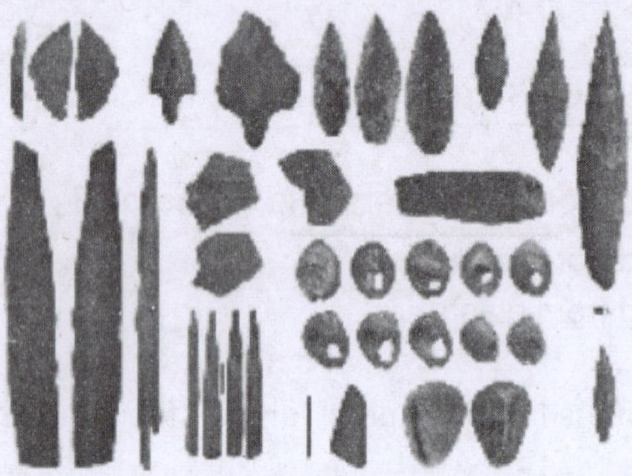

(a) Old stone age tools
(b) Old stone age vessels
(c) Old stone age containers
(d) Old stone age paintings

8. **When there was no proper house and building in the ancient times, where did the early man lived?**

(a) On branches of trees (b) Caves
(c) Beside river (d) Both (a) and (b)

9. **Choose the correct option(s) defining Hominins.**

(a) Early human beings (b) Plants
(c) Animals (d) All of these

10. **We know so much about the early humans. From where do we get information about their life?**

(a) Paintings
(b) Bones and tools
(c) Remains of shelter
(d) All of the above

11. Choose the odd one out.

(a) Hunters
(b) Gatherers
(c) Nomads
(d) Tribes

12. .... are the places, where evidences of existence of early human beings were found.

(a) Paintings
(b) Caves
(c) Archealogical sites and remains
(d) Excavations

13. Complete the given analogy.

Bhimbetka : ? :: Ajanta Ellora : Maharashtra

(a) Rajasthan
(b) Madhya Pradesh
(c) Odisha
(d) Uttar Pradesh

14. What does a person who gives us information about past through excavations of sites called?

(a) Historians
(b) Archaeologist
(c) Astrologists
(d) None of the above

15. How early humans kept a record of their daily activities?

(a) By maintaining a record
(b) By drawing their daily activities on cave walls
(c) By writing a book
(d) All of the above

16. How many words given in the box are associated with the life of early human beings?

Nomads,	Farmers,	Settled life,	Caves,	Gatherers,	Towns,	Hunters

(a) Six
(b) Four
(c) Seven
(d) Five

17. **In the following image, the early man is engaged in the activity of ....**

(a) ploughing (b) taming
(c) farming (d) fishing

18. **Identify the correct statement about the life of early humans from the following.**

(a) They ate the roots of plants and fruits from trees.
(b) They built proper houses.
(c) They used to travel by bus.
(d) They knew the art of cooking.

19. **Choose the correct statement.**

(a) Early humans used to wear synthetic and cotton clothes.
(b) Early humans used to practice agriculture on a large scale.
(c) Early humans used to get their foods from wild and domesticated animals.
(d) None of the above

20. **Match the following.**

List I	List II
A. Domestication	1. Cart without wheels
B. Hunters	2. Rearing animal for milk, meat and eggs
C. Sledge	3. Killing animals or birds for meat

Codes

	A	B	C		A	B	C
(a)	3	1	2	(b)	2	1	3
(c)	2	3	1	(d)	1	2	3

21. **Read the following statements and select which ones are true (T) and which ones are false (F).**

I. **Early humans were aware of science and technology.**

II. **Stone age was a period when humans made tools and weapons of copper.**

Codes

	I	II
(a)	T	F
(b)	F	F
(c)	F	T
(d)	T	T

22. **Unscramble the letters given in the options to obtain the name of famous cave in India which is found in Maharashtra.**

(a) BAMIDA
(b) ELLRAO
(c) VADNAP
(d) None of these

Darken your choice with HB Pencil

1.	ⓐ ⓑ ⓒ ⓓ	5.	ⓐ ⓑ ⓒ ⓓ	9.	ⓐ ⓑ ⓒ ⓓ	13.	ⓐ ⓑ ⓒ ⓓ	17.	ⓐ ⓑ ⓒ ⓓ	21.	ⓐ ⓑ ⓒ ⓓ
2.	ⓐ ⓑ ⓒ ⓓ	6.	ⓐ ⓑ ⓒ ⓓ	10.	ⓐ ⓑ ⓒ ⓓ	14.	ⓐ ⓑ ⓒ ⓓ	18.	ⓐ ⓑ ⓒ ⓓ	22.	ⓐ ⓑ ⓒ ⓓ
3.	ⓐ ⓑ ⓒ ⓓ	7.	ⓐ ⓑ ⓒ ⓓ	11.	ⓐ ⓑ ⓒ ⓓ	15.	ⓐ ⓑ ⓒ ⓓ	19.	ⓐ ⓑ ⓒ ⓓ		
4.	ⓐ ⓑ ⓒ ⓓ	8.	ⓐ ⓑ ⓒ ⓓ	12.	ⓐ ⓑ ⓒ ⓓ	16.	ⓐ ⓑ ⓒ ⓓ	20.	ⓐ ⓑ ⓒ ⓓ		

05

The Story of Fire and Beginning of Settled Life

MCQs 1 Mark Questions

1. What was the main discovery by early man which changed the way of their living?

(a) Fire (b) Transport (c) Clothing (d) Farming

2. How the early humans discovered fire?

(a) By using natural gas (b) By striking stones

(c) By matchsticks (d) By burning kerosene

3. The early human beings lived in jungle where there were so many animals. How did the early humans used to frightened the animals?

(a) By pelting stone (b) By making sounds

(c) By using stone weapons (d) By using torch of fire

4. Before the discovery of fire, the early man used to eat which type of food?

(a) Cooked food (b) Raw food

(c) Both (a) and (b) (d) None of these

5. Look at the picture given below and identify what exactly the early man is trying to do.

(a) He is preparing his food (b) He is making fire

(c) He is making tools (d) He is just sitting and relaxing

6. How did early humans discovered that plants can grow?

(a) By accidentally throwing seeds in the soil
(b) By planting trees
(c) Practicing farming
(d) All of these

7 Why did early humans settled near water bodies?

(a) They liked to stay near water.
(b) They were always thirsty.
(c) The use of water helped them to grow more crops.
(d) None of the above

8. How did early man realised that they could also cross rivers?

(a) By using boats
(b) By swimming
(c) By seeing logs of wood floating in water
(d) All of the above

9. Look at the picture given below and answer what is this object.

(a) Raft
(b) Boat
(c) Sledge
(d) Ship

10. Choose the odd one out.

(a) Raft
(b) Sledge
(c) Wheel
(d) Cart

11. Which of the following animals were first domesticated by humans?

(a) Goats and horse
(b) Elephant and donkey
(c) Goats and dogs
(d) Cows and sheep

12. Which was the first animal to be domesticated by early humans?

(a) Cat
(b) Horse
(c) Dog
(d) Pig

13. **Why did the early human relocate from one place to another?**
(a) For better career opportunities and growth.
(b) For searching the supply of freshwater.
(c) For growing crops on a more fertile lands.
(d) Both (b) and (c)

14. **Which of the following was the most remarkable invention of the early humans?**
(a) Wheel (b) Pottery (c) Paintings (d) Rafts

15. **As the early man civilised, he started eating cooked food. What did he used to cook his food?**
(a) Fire (b) Pots (c) Wood blocks (d) Both (a) and (b)

16. **The wheel used by early man for pottery was known as ....**
(a) potter's wheel (b) sledge wheel
(c) raft wheel (d) None of these

17. **Choose the correct order that describes the various ways to produce fire since the beginning of mankind.**
I. Matchsticks **II. Stones**
III. Lighter
Codes
(a) I, II, III (b) III, II, I
(c) II, I, III (d) I, III, II

18. **Identify the correct statement.**
(a) Early man used sharpened stones as their tools for hunting.
(b) Early man discovered fire which was not useful.
(c) Early man used to live in proper houses.
(d) All of the above

19. **Match the following.**

	List I		List II
A.	Bullocks	1.	Tamed for milk
B.	Cows and goats	2.	To plough the field for farming
C.	Sledge	3.	To guard domesticated animals
D.	Dogs	4.	A vehicle drawn by horses and dogs

Codes

	A	B	C	D
(a)	1	2	3	4
(b)	2	1	4	3
(c)	2	4	1	3
(d)	2	3	4	1

20. Read the following statements and select which ones are true (T) and which ones are false (F).

I. Early humans domesticated animals only for milk.

II. Early humans preferred to live near lakes and rivers.

Codes

	I	II
(a)	F	F
(b)	T	T
(c)	F	T
(d)	T	F

21. Read the statements given below and identify the correct option.

I. Animals which provided food and could be used to carry loads.

II. Places where early humans started living for long period of time.

	I	II
(a)	Domestic animals	Settlements
(b)	Wild animals	Rafts
(c)	Animals	Sledges
(d)	Dogs	Caves

22. Unscramble the letters given in the options to find out the name of the invention which was used by early human beings for pottery and transportation.

(a) ELHWE (b) FART

(c) OABT (d) None of these

Darken your choice with HB Pencil

1.	ⓐ ⓑ ⓒ ⓓ	5.	ⓐ ⓑ ⓒ ⓓ	9.	ⓐ ⓑ ⓒ ⓓ	13.	ⓐ ⓑ ⓒ ⓓ	17.	ⓐ ⓑ ⓒ ⓓ	21.	ⓐ ⓑ ⓒ ⓓ
2.	ⓐ ⓑ ⓒ ⓓ	6.	ⓐ ⓑ ⓒ ⓓ	10.	ⓐ ⓑ ⓒ ⓓ	14.	ⓐ ⓑ ⓒ ⓓ	18.	ⓐ ⓑ ⓒ ⓓ	22.	ⓐ ⓑ ⓒ ⓓ
3.	ⓐ ⓑ ⓒ ⓓ	7.	ⓐ ⓑ ⓒ ⓓ	11.	ⓐ ⓑ ⓒ ⓓ	15.	ⓐ ⓑ ⓒ ⓓ	19.	ⓐ ⓑ ⓒ ⓓ		
4.	ⓐ ⓑ ⓒ ⓓ	8.	ⓐ ⓑ ⓒ ⓓ	12.	ⓐ ⓑ ⓒ ⓓ	16.	ⓐ ⓑ ⓒ ⓓ	20.	ⓐ ⓑ ⓒ ⓓ		

06

Means of Transport and Communication

MCQs 1 Mark Questions

1. Which of the following animals is/are used as means of transport in ancient times?

(a) Horses (b) Deer
(c) Camels (d) Both (a) and (c)

2. Which of the following animals is/are also known as beasts of burden?

(a) Camels (b) Dogs (c) Donkeys (d) Both (a) and (c)

3. Why bus is significant means of road transport for many peoples?

(a) It is affordable.
(b) It can be used for transporting machines.
(c) It is fastest means of transport.
(d) None of the above

4. Raj wanted to travel out of country. Which of the following will be the best mode of transport for him?

(a) Bus (b) Train (c) Cycle (d) Aeroplane

5. Identify the meaning of the road sign shown in the picture given below.

(a) Narrow bridge ahead (b) No crossing
(c) Wide road ahead (d) Two way traffic

6. Which of the following is the costly mode of transportation?

(a) Aeroplanes (b) Trains
(c) Waterways (d) Railways

7. Identify the means of water transport which is made up of wood.

(a) Raft (b) Truck (c) Van (d) Ship

8. Which of the following is the cheapest means of transport in India?

(a) Airways (b) Railways
(c) Waterways (d) Roadways

9. Who is associated with the discovery of fastest means of transportation?

(a) Thomas Edison (b) Wright Brothers
(c) Marconi (d) JL Baird

10. Which among the following road signs means zebra crossing ahead?

(a) 
(b) 
(c) 
(d) 

11. Sharing or exchanging messages, information or ideas with one another is called ....

(a) communication (b) movement
(c) talking (d) None of these

12. Which among the following ways helped the early man to communicate with each other?

(a) Signs and Signals (b) Paintings
(c) Drawings (d) All of these

13. Riya wants to send the message to her grandparents. What will be the fastest way to send the message?

(a) Speed post (b) Telegram
(c) E-mail (d) Postcard

14. Choose the odd one out.

(a) Fax (b) Letter
(c) Telephone (d) Notepad

15. Ram has to give information to a large number of people. Which of the following will be the best mode of communication for him?

(a) Newspaper (b) Radio
(c) Television (d) All of these

16. What is the full form of SMS?

(a) Small Messaging Service
(b) Small Means of Service
(c) Short Messaging Service
(d) Short Message Service

17. What is/are the use(s) of satellites?

(a) To view live telecast of an event. (b) For making crafts.
(c) For printing of newspapers. (d) None of these

18. Complete the given analogy.

Personal Communication : Letters :: Mass Communication : ?

(a) Postcard (b) Fax
(c) Radio (d) Telephone

19. From the given words in box, identify how many of them are personal means of communication.

Newspapers, Magazines, Letters, Radio, Telephones, E-mails, Television, Smartphones

(a) Seven (b) Three
(c) Four (d) Six

20. Choose the correct statement from the given options.

(a) To travel short distance, we go on foot.
(b) Buses are faster means of transport as compared to trains.
(c) Early men used to travel by public transport.
(d) All of the above

21. Unscramble the letters given in the options to find out the name of the fastest means of transport.

(a) CICYEBL (b) TGONA

(c) OREAPALEN (d) AWLSIYAR

22. Choose the incorrect statement(s) about ship.

I. It can carry people and goods to far off places.

II. It has more than 100 wheels which help it to float.

Codes

(a) Only I (b) Only II

(c) Both (a) and (b) (d) Neither I nor II

23. Identify the incorrectly matched pair.

(a) Computer — Internet

(b) Mass Communication — Radio

(c) Video Message — Fax

(d) Television — Entertainment

24. Unscramble the letters given in the options to find out the name of the mode of transportation with the help of information given below.

A watercraft which can travels over land, water or ice.

(a) BUSRAMENI (b) EROVHARFCT

(c) OBTA (d) None of these

25. Match the following.

List I	List II
A. Aeroplane	1. Bird used for communication in ancient days
B. Pigeon	2. Fastest means of transport
C. Mobiles	3. Means of transport on water
D. Boats	4. Modern means of communication

Codes

	A	B	C	D		A	B	C	D
(a)	2	3	4	1	(b)	2	4	1	3
(c)	2	1	4	3	(d)	2	3	1	4

26. Read the following statements and identify the correct option.

I. I can only run on a special track.

II. I sail through the sea.

	I	III
(a)	Truck	Boat
(b)	Train	Ship
(c)	Cycle	Fish
(d)	Boat	Ship

27. Read the following statements and select which ones are true(T) and which ones are false(F).

I. Through SMS, we can send the messages instantly.

II. In ancient days, people used to communicate through fax.

Codes

	I	II
(a)	T	T
(b)	F	F
(c)	T	F
(d)	F	T

Darken your choice with HB Pencil

1.	ⓐ ⓑ ⓒ ⓓ	6.	ⓐ ⓑ ⓒ ⓓ	11.	ⓐ ⓑ ⓒ ⓓ	16.	ⓐ ⓑ ⓒ ⓓ	21.	ⓐ ⓑ ⓒ ⓓ	26.	ⓐ ⓑ ⓒ ⓓ
2.	ⓐ ⓑ ⓒ ⓓ	7.	ⓐ ⓑ ⓒ ⓓ	12.	ⓐ ⓑ ⓒ ⓓ	17.	ⓐ ⓑ ⓒ ⓓ	22.	ⓐ ⓑ ⓒ ⓓ	27.	ⓐ ⓑ ⓒ ⓓ
3.	ⓐ ⓑ ⓒ ⓓ	8.	ⓐ ⓑ ⓒ ⓓ	13.	ⓐ ⓑ ⓒ ⓓ	18.	ⓐ ⓑ ⓒ ⓓ	23.	ⓐ ⓑ ⓒ ⓓ		
4.	ⓐ ⓑ ⓒ ⓓ	9.	ⓐ ⓑ ⓒ ⓓ	14.	ⓐ ⓑ ⓒ ⓓ	19.	ⓐ ⓑ ⓒ ⓓ	24.	ⓐ ⓑ ⓒ ⓓ		
5.	ⓐ ⓑ ⓒ ⓓ	10.	ⓐ ⓑ ⓒ ⓓ	15.	ⓐ ⓑ ⓒ ⓓ	20.	ⓐ ⓑ ⓒ ⓓ	25.	ⓐ ⓑ ⓒ ⓓ		

07

Our Heritage (Dance, Festivals, Epics and Musical Instruments)

MCQs 1 Mark Questions

1. Which term is used for the history, culture and tradition that forms the character of a society?
   (a) Heritage (b) Buildings (c) Traditions (d) Monuments

2. What is the characteristic of Indian culture?
   (a) Poor and diverse (b) Rich and diverse
   (c) Diverse and advance (d) Simple and advance

3. Which dance form has its origin in Northern India?
   (a) Odissi (b) Manipuri (c) Kathak (d) Bihu

4. Complete the given analogy.
   Padma Subrahmanyam : Bharatnatyam :: Birju Maharaj : ?
   (a) Manipuri (b) Odissi (c) Kathak (d) Kathakali

5. Identify which dance form is shown in the picture given below.

   (a) Kathak (b) Odissi (c) Bharatnatyam (d) Kathakali

6. Which of the following dance forms belongs to Southern part?
   (a) Kathak (b) Odissi (c) Manipuri (d) Salsa

7. Who among the following is the famous Bharatnatyam dancer?

(a) Rukmini Devi (b) Uday Shankar
(c) Savitha Sastry (d) None of these

8. Identify the National Festival(s) of our country.

(a) Independence Day (b) Republic Day
(c) Gandhi Jayanti (d) All of the above

9. During the festival of Dusshera, we burn the effigies of which of the following?

(a) Ravana (b) Khumbhakaran
(c) Vibhishana (d) Both (a) and (b)

10. Complete the given analogy.
Pongal : Tamil Nadu :: ? : Kerala

(a) Eid (b) Basant Panchami
(c) Onam (d) Buddh Purnima

11. Identify the incorrect statement regarding the festival Eid.

(a) People offer Namaz (b) They eat sewain
(c) They wear new clothes (d) None of these

12. The famous festival Navroz belongs to which of the following communities of India?

(a) Hindus (b) Sikhs
(c) Muslims (d) Parsis

13. During which festival the people worship cow and prepare rice with milk and jaggery?

(a) Onam (b) Eid (c) Pongal (d) Diwali

14. Identify the major festival(s) of North India.

(a) Diwali (b) Dusshera
(c) Holi (d) All of these

15. How many cultural festivals are mentioned in the box?

Holi, Independence Day, Diwali, Pongal, Republic Day, Onam, Dusshera, Basant Panchami, Eid, Gurupurab

(a) Seven (b) Eight
(c) Four (d) Six

16. **How many languages are mentioned in the Indian Constitution?**

(a) 23 (b) 24
(c) 22 (d) 25

17. **Identify the main language spoken in the Eastern part of India.**

(a) Bengali (b) Telugu
(c) Punjabi (d) Urdu

18. **Identify memorial which is dedicated to Gandhiji.**

(a) Red fort (b) Rajghat
(c) Qutub Minar (d) Jallianwala Bagh

19. **What are the two styles of classical music?**

(a) Dhrupad, Jazz (b) Carnatic, Jazz
(c) Hindustani, Carnatic (d) Pop, Carnatic

20. **Who among the following is associated with the instrument mentioned in the picture?**

(a) Birju Maharaj (b) Zakir Hussain
(c) Guru Gangadhar (d) Mrinalini Sarabhai

21. **Here are the name of some musical instruments in the box, identify how many among them are used in Hindustani style of music.**

Sarangi, Tanpura, Violin, Veena, Sitar, Harmonium, Dholak, Guitar, Tabla, Ghatam, Tambourine

(a) Six (b) Seven
(c) Nine (d) Eight

22. **Identify the correct statement(s).**

(a) The people in the Southern states of India speaks Punjabi.
(b) Different languages are spoken across the nation.
(c) We can only speak Hindi in India.
(d) All of the above

23. **Identify the incorrectly matched pair.**

(a) Kathak- Uttar Pradesh (b) Bihu- Assam
(c) Odissi- Odisha (d) Kuchipudi- Kerala

24. **Choose the incorrectly matched pair.**

(a) Gurupurab- Sikhs (b) Diwali- Hindus
(c) Eid- Muslims (d) Navratri- Gujaratis

25. **Unscramble the letters given in the options to find out the name of the month that is associated with the festival of Eid.**

(a) SUATGU (b) CTBOEOR
(c) EBMDERCE (d) None of these

26. **Match the following.**

List I	List II
A. Carnatic	1. Musical instrument
B. Harmonium	2. Classical music of India
C. Shovana Narayan	3. Kathak dancer

Codes

	A	B	C		A	B	C
(a)	2	3	1	(b)	2	1	3
(c)	1	2	3	(d)	3	1	2

27. **Read the following statements and select which ones are true (T) and which ones are false (F).**

I. India is a land of festivals.

II. We only celebrate National Festivals in India.

Codes

	I	II		I	II
(a)	F	F	(b)	T	T
(c)	T	F	(d)	F	T

Darken your choice with HB Pencil

1. ⓐ ⓑ ⓒ ⓓ	6. ⓐ ⓑ ⓒ ⓓ	11. ⓐ ⓑ ⓒ ⓓ	16. ⓐ ⓑ ⓒ ⓓ	21. ⓐ ⓑ ⓒ ⓓ	26. ⓐ ⓑ ⓒ ⓓ
2. ⓐ ⓑ ⓒ ⓓ	7. ⓐ ⓑ ⓒ ⓓ	12. ⓐ ⓑ ⓒ ⓓ	17. ⓐ ⓑ ⓒ ⓓ	22. ⓐ ⓑ ⓒ ⓓ	27. ⓐ ⓑ ⓒ ⓓ
3. ⓐ ⓑ ⓒ ⓓ	8. ⓐ ⓑ ⓒ ⓓ	13. ⓐ ⓑ ⓒ ⓓ	18. ⓐ ⓑ ⓒ ⓓ	23. ⓐ ⓑ ⓒ ⓓ	
4. ⓐ ⓑ ⓒ ⓓ	9. ⓐ ⓑ ⓒ ⓓ	14. ⓐ ⓑ ⓒ ⓓ	19. ⓐ ⓑ ⓒ ⓓ	24. ⓐ ⓑ ⓒ ⓓ	
5. ⓐ ⓑ ⓒ ⓓ	10. ⓐ ⓑ ⓒ ⓓ	15. ⓐ ⓑ ⓒ ⓓ	20. ⓐ ⓑ ⓒ ⓓ	25. ⓐ ⓑ ⓒ ⓓ	

08

Our Country (States of India)

MCQs 1 Mark Questions

1. **India is situated in .... part of the continent of Asia.**
   (a) Northern
   (b) Southern
   (c) Eastern
   (d) Western

2. **Which among the following is not included in the physical features of India?**
   (a) Mountain Ranges
   (b) Plateau
   (c) Desert
   (d) Climate

3. **Identify the place which is surrounded by water from all sides.**
   (a) Ocean
   (b) Sea
   (c) River
   (d) Island

4. **Complete the given analogy.**
   Lakshadweep : Arabian Sea :: Andaman and Nicobar : ?
   (a) Bay of Bengal
   (b) Deccan Plateau
   (c) Desert
   (d) None of these

5. **On which date 'Jana-gana-mana' adopted as the National Anthem of India?**
   (a) 26th January, 1950
   (b) 24th January, 1950
   (c) 26th January, 1949
   (d) 15th August, 1947

6. **What is the term used for the objects, signs or symbols that represent a country?**
   (a) Cultural symbols
   (b) Heritage symbols
   (c) National symbols
   (d) Identity symbols

7. **The National Song, Vande Matram has been taken from which of the following novels?**
   (a) Joshi Math
   (b) Anand Math
   (c) Neel Darpan
   (d) None of these

8. Which of the following animals is not included in our National Emblem?

(a) Camel (b) Horse
(c) Bull (d) Elephant

9. What does the National Emblem of India symbolise?

(a) Power (b) Confidence
(c) Courage (d) All of these

10. Name the project started by the government to increase the population of our National Animal Tiger.

(a) Save Tiger Project (b) Project Tiger
(c) Project National Animal (d) None of these

11. Choose the incorrect statement(s) about the language of India.

(a) Hindi is the national language.
(b) India does not have a national language.
(c) Hindi and English are our official language.
(d) None of the above

12. Which of the following is/are the Western states of India?

(a) Karnataka (b) Gujarat
(c) Maharashtra (d) All of these

13. Choose the odd one out.

(a) Bhopal (b) Raipur
(c) Jaipur (d) Tamil Nadu

14. Identify the Northern State of India from the given options.

(a) Kerala
(b) Tamil Nadu
(c) Karnataka
(d) Uttar Pradesh

15. What does the wheel in the National Flag symbolise?

(a) Swadeshi Movement
(b) Constant Movement
(c) Both (a) and (b)
(d) Satyagraha Movement

16. **How many Union Territories are mentioned in the box given below?**

Chandigarh, Rajasthan, Puducherry, Sikkim, Nagaland, Jammu and Kashmir, Delhi, Ladakh, Madhya Pradesh, Daman and Diu

(a) Seven (b) Eight
(c) Six (d) Nine

17. **There are three colours in National Flag of India. Choose the correct pair(s) with relation to the significance of the colour.**

(a) Saffron — Strength and courage (b) White — Anger
(c) Green — Agricultural land (d) All of these

18. **Choose the incorrectly matched pair.**

(a) Lakshadweep — Kavaratti
(b) Chandigarh — Silvassa
(c) Andaman and Nicobar Island — Port Blair
(d) Goa — Panaji

19. **Identify the correct statement(s) regarding the hoisting of National Flag in India.**

I. **The Saffron band of the flag should always be on top when the flag is unfurled.**

II. **The flag must be hoisted after sunrise and must be brought down just before sunset.**

Codes

(a) Only I (b) Only II
(c) Both I and II (d) None of these

20. **Match the following.**

List I (States)	List II (Capital)
A. West Bengal	1. Kolkata
B. Sikkim	2. Gangtok
C. Nagaland	3. Kohima

Codes

	A	B	C		A	B	C
(a)	1	2	3	(b)	2	3	1
(c)	2	1	3	(d)	1	3	2

21. Read the following statements and select which ones are true (T) and which ones are false (F).

I. Our national song is composed by Bankim Chandra Chatterjee.

II. The national fruit is found in countries with tropical monsoon seasons.

Codes

	I	II		I	II
(a)	T	T	(b)	T	F
(c)	F	F	(d)	F	T

22. Unscramble the letters given in the options to find out the name of the place with the help of information given below.

It is a Union Territory of India.

Codes

(a) CKOWNUL

(b) LEHDI

(c) KIMISK

(d) None of the above

Darken your choice with HB Pencil

1.	ⓐ ⓑ ⓒ ⓓ	5.	ⓐ ⓑ ⓒ ⓓ	9.	ⓐ ⓑ ⓒ ⓓ	13.	ⓐ ⓑ ⓒ ⓓ	17.	ⓐ ⓑ ⓒ ⓓ	21.	ⓐ ⓑ ⓒ ⓓ
2.	ⓐ ⓑ ⓒ ⓓ	6.	ⓐ ⓑ ⓒ ⓓ	10.	ⓐ ⓑ ⓒ ⓓ	14.	ⓐ ⓑ ⓒ ⓓ	18.	ⓐ ⓑ ⓒ ⓓ	22.	ⓐ ⓑ ⓒ ⓓ
3.	ⓐ ⓑ ⓒ ⓓ	7.	ⓐ ⓑ ⓒ ⓓ	11.	ⓐ ⓑ ⓒ ⓓ	15.	ⓐ ⓑ ⓒ ⓓ	19.	ⓐ ⓑ ⓒ ⓓ		
4.	ⓐ ⓑ ⓒ ⓓ	8.	ⓐ ⓑ ⓒ ⓓ	12.	ⓐ ⓑ ⓒ ⓓ	16.	ⓐ ⓑ ⓒ ⓓ	20.	ⓐ ⓑ ⓒ ⓓ		

09

Four Metro Cities

MCQs 1 Mark Questions

1. **Which of the following cities was formed by merging of seven Islands?**
(a) Mumbai (b) Kolkata (c) Delhi (d) Chennai

2. **What is most popular festival of Mumbai?**
(a) Onam (b) Ganesh Chaturthi (c) Navaratri (d) Pongal

3. **Which of the following monuments is located in Mumbai?**

(a) 

(b) 

(c) 

(d) 

4. **Complete the given analogy.**
Mumbai : ? :: Delhi : Political Capital of India
(a) Social Capital of India (b) Commercial Capital of India
(c) Cultural Capital of India (d) None of these

5. **Which among the following monuments was built in 1887 in Mumbai to mark the golden jubilee of Queen of Britain?**
(a) Victoria Terminus (b) Gateway of India
(c) India Gate (d) The Elephanta Caves

6. **Delhi is situated on the banks of which of the following rivers?**
(a) Ganga (b) Godavari (c) Yamuna (d) Tapi

7. Who among the following planned the city of New Delhi?

(a) John Nash (b) Edwin Lutyens
(c) Herbert Baker (d) None of these

8. Identify the monument which was built by Shah Jahan, located in Delhi.

(a) 

(b) 

(c) 

(d) 

9. Which type of climate is experienced by Delhi?

(a) Continental (b) Dry (c) Extreme (d) Temperate

10. What is the name of Indira Gandhi's Samadhi which is located in Delhi?

(a) Raj Ghat (b) Shakti Sthal (c) Shantivan (d) Vir Bhumi

11. Look at the picture given below and identify the name of the temple located in Delhi.

(a) Kapaleeshwarar Temple (b) Meenakshi Temple
(c) Ashtalakshmi Temple (d) None of these

12. Riya tells Rahul that she is visiting the 'city of joy'. Which city is she referring to?

(a) Delhi (b) Kolkata
(c) Chennai (d) Mumbai

13. Kolkata is main centre of which of the following industries?

(a) Jute (b) Textile

(c) Cotton (d) Both (a) and (b)

14. Where is the monument Belur Math, established by Swami Vivekananda located?

(a) Delhi (b) Mumbai

(c) Kolkata (d) Chennai

15. Which among the following cities was the first to have an underground railway system called the metro?

(a) Delhi (b) Mumbai

(c) Kolkata (d) Chennai

16. Identify the name of the bridge in Kolkata shown in the picture given below.

(a) Vidyasagar Setu (b) Rabindra Setu

(c) Nehru Setu (d) None of these

17. Complete the given analogy.

Maharashtra : Mumbai :: West Bengal : ?

(a) Kolkata (b) Delhi (c) Assam (d) Gujarat

18. In which part of India, the city of Chennai is located?

(a) Eastern (b) Northern (c) Southern (d) Western

19. Choose the odd one out.

(a) Delhi (b) Kolkata (c) Gujarat (d) Mumbai

20. Choose the correct statement(s) about Marine Drive.

I. It is located in Delhi.

II. It is also known as Queen's Necklace.

Codes

(a) Only I (b) Only II

(c) Both I and II (d) Neither I nor II

21. Read the following statements and choose the correct statement(s) about Kolkata.
(a) It became the capital of British India in 1772.
(b) It is a major port town of India.
(c) The first modern university was founded here in 1857.
(d) All of the above

22. Match the following.

List I	List II
A. Diamond Harbour	1. Delhi
B. Fort Saint George	2. Mumbai
C. Juhu Beach	3. Chennai
D. Saint James Church	4. Kolkata

Codes

	A	B	C	D		A	B	C	D
(a)	1	3	2	4	(b)	4	3	2	1
(c)	4	3	1	2	(d)	1	3	4	2

23. Unscramble the letters given in the options to find out the name of the popular personality who composed the National Anthem.
(a) BIRKA
(b) LIAKSADA
(c) BINARDARTNAH ATOGER
(d) None of these

24. Read the following statements and select which ones are true (T) and which ones are false (F).
I. Bhabha Atomic Research Centre is situated in Chennai.
II. The India Gate was designed by Edwin Lutyens.

Codes

	I	II		I	II
(a)	F	F	(b)	F	T
(c)	T	F	(d)	T	T

Darken your choice with HB Pencil

1. ⓐ ⓑ ⓒ ⓓ	5. ⓐ ⓑ ⓒ ⓓ	9. ⓐ ⓑ ⓒ ⓓ	13. ⓐ ⓑ ⓒ ⓓ	17. ⓐ ⓑ ⓒ ⓓ	21. ⓐ ⓑ ⓒ ⓓ
2. ⓐ ⓑ ⓒ ⓓ	6. ⓐ ⓑ ⓒ ⓓ	10. ⓐ ⓑ ⓒ ⓓ	14. ⓐ ⓑ ⓒ ⓓ	18. ⓐ ⓑ ⓒ ⓓ	22. ⓐ ⓑ ⓒ ⓓ
3. ⓐ ⓑ ⓒ ⓓ	7. ⓐ ⓑ ⓒ ⓓ	11. ⓐ ⓑ ⓒ ⓓ	15. ⓐ ⓑ ⓒ ⓓ	19. ⓐ ⓑ ⓒ ⓓ	23. ⓐ ⓑ ⓒ ⓓ
4. ⓐ ⓑ ⓒ ⓓ	8. ⓐ ⓑ ⓒ ⓓ	12. ⓐ ⓑ ⓒ ⓓ	16. ⓐ ⓑ ⓒ ⓓ	20. ⓐ ⓑ ⓒ ⓓ	24. ⓐ ⓑ ⓒ ⓓ

10

People Who Help Us

MCQs 1 Mark Questions

1. Who protects country from the attacks of the enemy?
   (a) Firefighters
   (b) Doctors
   (c) Soldiers
   (d) Policeman

2. Identify the incorrectly matched pair.
   (a) Teacher – School
   (b) Doctor – Hospital
   (c) Postman – Post Office
   (d) Police – Railway Station

3. Who among the following repairs lights, fans and wires?
   (a) Plumber
   (b) Electrician
   (c) Postman
   (d) Carpenter

4. The teacher always helps us to become ....
   (a) responsible
   (b) better person
   (c) knowledgeable
   (d) All of these

5. What is/are the role(s) of teachers?
   (a) They teach us to work together and be punctual.
   (b) They make food for us in school.
   (c) They teach us to read and write.
   (d) Both (a) and (c)

6. If the building catches fire who will rescue all the person caught in fire?
   (a) Firemen
   (b) Soldier
   (c) Doctor
   (d) Carpenter

7. We all have tables and chairs in our home. Identify the person who makes it for us.
   (a) Cobbler
   (b) Farmer
   (c) Carpenter
   (d) Doctor

8. **Who looks after the drainage system in the house?**
(a) Electrician (b) Plumber
(c) Carpenter (d) Cobbler

9. **A person who knows the art of sewing and stitching is known as ....**
(a) cobbler (b) tailor
(c) carpenter (d) plumber

10. **Who among the following maintains law and order in the society?**
(a) Judge (b) Police
(c) Farmer (d) Both (a) and (b)

11. **Which among the following is/are the duty/duties of farmers?**
(a) Sowing the seeds (b) Giving fertiliser
(c) Taking care of the field (d) All of these

12. **Complete the given analogy.**
Lawyer : ? :: TTE : Railway Station
(a) Court (b) Fire Station (c) Police Station (d) School

13. **Who among the following is/are the community helper(s)?**
(a) Doctors (b) Teachers (c) Policemen (d) All of these

14. **What is not the duty of firefighters?**
(a) To rescue the sick and injured
(b) To operate fire equipment.
(c) To leave the injured person and only focus on extinguishing fire.
(d) Both (a) and (b)

15. **The main occupation of the people living near the sea is ....**
(a) gardening (b) cooking (c) mining (d) fishing

16. **Choose the odd one out.**
(a) Doctor (b) Surgeon (c) Pharmacist (d) Lawyer

17. **Identify the correct statement about community workers.**
(a) They do not help the poor people.
(b) They should not be respected.
(c) They are a very important part of our society.
(d) None of the above

18. Which among the following statements is incorrect about community?

(a) It is a group of people living together.

(b) People living in community do not help each other.

(c) People living in a community are always ready to help.

(d) None of the above

19. Which among the following statements is incorrect about sweeper?

(a) He keeps the roads, parks and other places clean.

(b) He uses specialised machines and equipments for sweeping.

(c) He is an important part of our community.

(d) None of the above

20. Choose the incorrect statement(s).

I. We should always cooperate with the police because they work day and night to keep us protected.

II. We go to shopkeeper to buy all the things we need.

Codes

(a) Only I

(b) Only II

(c) Both I and II

(d) Neither I nor II

21. Read the given statements and select which ones are true (T) and which ones are false (F).

I. The tailors use pipe wrench to stitch the clothes.

II. The doctors use stethoscope to check patients.

Codes

	I	II
(a)	F	F
(b)	T	F
(c)	F	T
(d)	T	T

22. Unscramble the letters given in options to find out the name of a person who repairs our shoes.

(a) IATOLR

(b) OPIELC

(c) ERLBCOB

(d) HATEECR

23. **Match the following.**

List I	List II
A. Chef	1. Chalk
B. Barber	2. Scissors
C. Teacher	3. Ladle

Codes

	A	B	C		A	B	C
(a)	1	2	3	(b)	2	1	3
(c)	3	2	1	(d)	2	3	1

24. **Read the following statements and select which ones are true (T) and which ones are false (F).**

I. A plumber makes wooden furniture for us.

II. Farmers are an important part of our community.

Codes

	I	II
(a)	T	F
(b)	F	F
(c)	F	T
(d)	T	T

Darken your choice with HB Pencil

1. ⓐ ⓑ ⓒ ⓓ	5. ⓐ ⓑ ⓒ ⓓ	9. ⓐ ⓑ ⓒ ⓓ	13. ⓐ ⓑ ⓒ ⓓ	17. ⓐ ⓑ ⓒ ⓓ	21. ⓐ ⓑ ⓒ ⓓ
2. ⓐ ⓑ ⓒ ⓓ	6. ⓐ ⓑ ⓒ ⓓ	10. ⓐ ⓑ ⓒ ⓓ	14. ⓐ ⓑ ⓒ ⓓ	18. ⓐ ⓑ ⓒ ⓓ	22. ⓐ ⓑ ⓒ ⓓ
3. ⓐ ⓑ ⓒ ⓓ	7. ⓐ ⓑ ⓒ ⓓ	11. ⓐ ⓑ ⓒ ⓓ	15. ⓐ ⓑ ⓒ ⓓ	19. ⓐ ⓑ ⓒ ⓓ	23. ⓐ ⓑ ⓒ ⓓ
4. ⓐ ⓑ ⓒ ⓓ	8. ⓐ ⓑ ⓒ ⓓ	12. ⓐ ⓑ ⓒ ⓓ	16. ⓐ ⓑ ⓒ ⓓ	20. ⓐ ⓑ ⓒ ⓓ	24. ⓐ ⓑ ⓒ ⓓ

Practice Set 01

Time : 60 Mins. Max. Marks : 35

General Instructions

1. This question paper contains 35 questions.
2. Each question carries 1 mark.
3. All questions are compulsory. There is no negative marking.
4. Use HB pencil / Blue ball point pen to mark your choice of answer by darkening the circles on the OMR Sheet.

1. Which among the following is/are part of the Solar System?

(a) Asteroids (b) Sun
(c) Planets (d) All of these

2. Identify the factor(s) on which the life on the Earth is possible.

(a) Air (b) Temperature
(c) Soil (d) All of these

3. Which of the following is not dependent on air for their movement?

(a) Birds (b) Metro train
(c) Aeroplane (d) Parachute

4. Complete the given analogy.

Excess of rainfall : Flood : : Shortage of rainfall : ?

(a) Flash flood (b) Drought
(c) Tsunami (d) Earthquake

5. Identify the planet, the rings of which are made up of ice, dust and rocks.

(a) Mars
(b) Saturn
(c) Jupiter
(d) None of the above

6. In how many days the moon completes one revolution around the Earth?

(a) 28 days (b) 27 days
(c) 24 days (d) 32 days

7. What is the interior molten area of the Earth called?

(a) Core
(b) Mantle
(c) Crust
(d) None of these

8. Which of the following oceans is located near India?

(a) Southern Ocean
(b) Arctic Ocean
(c) Atlantic Ocean
(d) Indian Ocean

9. The art of Bhimbetka caves are suitable examples of which of the following paintings?

(a) Abstract paintings
(b) Landscape paintings
(c) Cave paintings
(d) Modern painting

10. Identify the season in which weather is nice and days are sunny and it is certainly the best time to go to the beach.

(a) Summer
(b) Spring
(c) Winter
(d) Autumn

11. Choose the odd one out from the following sources of water.

(a) 

(b) 

(c) 

(d) 

12. Which of the following watercrafts can travel over land, water, mud and ice?

(a) Submarine
(b) Cruise
(c) Hovercraft
(d) Houseboat

13. Aryabhatta was the first artifical satellite launched by India in ....

(a) 1975 (b) 1970 (c) 1976 (d) 1979

14. Identify the mode of communication, which transmit information to the different parts of the world.

(a) Radio (b) Telephone (c) Mobile phone (d) All of these

15. Which of the following planets of Solar System takes almost 12 years to complete one revolution around the Sun?

(a) Neptune (b) Saturn (c) Jupiter (d) Mars

16. Identify the purpose(s) for which early man used stone tools.

(a) For cutting meat (b) For scraping bark from trees

(c) For chopping woods (d) All of these

17. Which of the following was not a distinctive feature of early humans?

(a) Ability to make and use simple tools.

(b) Ability to live in permanent settlement.

(c) Ability to create cave drawings.

(d) None of the above

18. For which of the following purpose(s) the early man migrated?

(a) In search of continuous supply of food grains.

(b) In search of continuous supply of potable water.

(c) Both (a) and (b)

(d) In search of continuous supply of stone tools.

19.

The object given in the picture above is one of the greatest invention of human kind. Initially this object was used for which of the following purposes?

(a) Pottery (b) Hunting

(c) Transportation (d) Painting

20. Kathakali is the popular dance form of which state of India?

(a) Tamil Nadu
(b) Kerala
(c) Manipur
(d) Uttar Pradesh

21. Identify the language which is not spoken in the Southern portion of India.

(a) Telugu
(b) Malayalam
(c) Tamil
(d) Nepali

22. Where is the famous Salar Jung Museum, Falaknuma Palace and Hussain Sagar Lake located?

(a) Bhopal
(b) Madurai
(c) Agra
(d) Hyderabad

23.

The image represents the parade of Republic Day. Where is this parade always take place in New Delhi?

(a) Gateway of India
(b) Janpath
(c) Rajpath
(d) Red fort

24. Identify correctly matched pair.

(a) Easter - Christian
(b) Lohri - Muslim
(c) Muharram - Sikhs
(d) Navroj - Hindus

25. During which festival the people worship cow and prepare rice with milk and jaggery?

(a) Eid
(b) Pongal
(c) Holi
(d) Diwali

26. Which festival marks the beginning of spring in India and is celebrated by worshipping Goddess Saraswati?

(a) Raksha Bandhan
(b) Navroj
(c) Basant Panchami
(d) Holi

27. The famous Eden Garden stadium is located in which of the following metro cities?

(a) Kolkata (b) Chennai
(c) Mumbai (d) Delhi

28. Name the garden which is located inside the premises of Rashtrapati Bhawan and opens for the public once in a year in the month of February.

(a) Shalimar Garden (b) Mughal Garden
(c) Jahanpanah City Forest (d) Garden of Five Senses

29. Which of the following beaches is/are located in Chennai?

(a) Marina Beach (b) Elliot's Beach
(c) Both (a) and (b) (d) Tajpur Beach

30. Where is the Jawaharlal Nehru University located in India?

(a) Mumbai (b) Kolkata
(c) Delhi (d) Chennai

31. Which among the following profession is considered as a symbol of power?

(a) Police (b) Doctor
(c) Teacher (d) Lawyer

32. Identify the incorrectly matched pair.

	State		Capital
(a)	Assam	–	Dispur
(b)	Nagaland	–	Kohima
(c)	Karnataka	–	Bengaluru
(d)	Odisha	–	Cuttack

33. Read the given statements and select which ones are true (T) and which ones are false (F).

I. Veterinary doctors treat sick people.

II. Traffic police is same as the general police.

Codes

	I	II		I	II
(a)	T	T	(b)	T	F
(c)	F	F	(d)	F	T

34. **Identify the correct statement(s).**

(a) Early humans lived at one place at a time and didn't move for anything.

(b) Early humans became food gatherer from food producers.

(c) Early humans used tools made of stones and bones.

(d) All of the above

35. **Match the following.**

	List I		List II
A.	Rajghat	1.	Samadhi of Indira Gandhi
B.	Shakti Sthal	2.	Samadhi of Gandhi ji
C.	Shantivan	3.	Samadhi of Lal Bahadur Shastri
D.	Vijayghat	4.	Samadhi of Pt Jawaharlal Nehru

Codes

	A	B	C	D		A	B	C	D
(a)	2	1	3	4	(b)	4	2	1	3
(c)	3	1	2	4	(d)	1	2	3	4

Darken your choice with HB Pencil

1.	ⓐ ⓑ ⓒ ⓓ	7.	ⓐ ⓑ ⓒ ⓓ	13.	ⓐ ⓑ ⓒ ⓓ	19.	ⓐ ⓑ ⓒ ⓓ	25.	ⓐ ⓑ ⓒ ⓓ	31.	ⓐ ⓑ ⓒ ⓓ
2.	ⓐ ⓑ ⓒ ⓓ	8.	ⓐ ⓑ ⓒ ⓓ	14.	ⓐ ⓑ ⓒ ⓓ	20.	ⓐ ⓑ ⓒ ⓓ	26.	ⓐ ⓑ ⓒ ⓓ	32.	ⓐ ⓑ ⓒ ⓓ
3.	ⓐ ⓑ ⓒ ⓓ	9.	ⓐ ⓑ ⓒ ⓓ	15.	ⓐ ⓑ ⓒ ⓓ	21.	ⓐ ⓑ ⓒ ⓓ	27.	ⓐ ⓑ ⓒ ⓓ	33.	ⓐ ⓑ ⓒ ⓓ
4.	ⓐ ⓑ ⓒ ⓓ	10.	ⓐ ⓑ ⓒ ⓓ	16.	ⓐ ⓑ ⓒ ⓓ	22.	ⓐ ⓑ ⓒ ⓓ	28.	ⓐ ⓑ ⓒ ⓓ	34.	ⓐ ⓑ ⓒ ⓓ
5.	ⓐ ⓑ ⓒ ⓓ	11.	ⓐ ⓑ ⓒ ⓓ	17.	ⓐ ⓑ ⓒ ⓓ	23.	ⓐ ⓑ ⓒ ⓓ	29.	ⓐ ⓑ ⓒ ⓓ	35.	ⓐ ⓑ ⓒ ⓓ
6.	ⓐ ⓑ ⓒ ⓓ	12.	ⓐ ⓑ ⓒ ⓓ	18.	ⓐ ⓑ ⓒ ⓓ	24.	ⓐ ⓑ ⓒ ⓓ	30.	ⓐ ⓑ ⓒ ⓓ		

Practice Set 02

Time : 60 Mins. Max. Marks : 35

General Instructions

1. This question paper contains 35 questions.
2. Each question carries 1 mark.
3. All questions are compulsory. There is no negative marking.
4. Use HB pencil / Blue ball point pen to mark your choice of answer by darkening the circles on the OMR Sheet.

MCQs 1 Mark Questions

1. Which planet of the Solar System takes 88 days to complete one orbit around the Sun?

(a) Mars (b) Jupiter (c) Mercury (d) Venus

2. What is/are the other name(s) of Constellation?

(a) Ursa Major (b) Ursa Minor
(c) Orian (d) All of the above

3. What are the large masses of the land on the Earth called?

(a) Oceans (b) Continents
(c) Lakes (d) Islands

4. Which of the following is/are the factor(s) responsible for air pollution?

(a) Smoke by factories (b) Harmful gases of vehicles
(c) Bursting fire crackers (d) All of these

5. The method of storing rainwater and reusing if for future use is called ....

(a) Rainwater storage (b) Rainwater harvesting
(c) Rainwater saving (d) Rainwater sustainability

6. Complete the analogy.

Brightest planet : Venus : : Darkest planet : ?

(a) Mercury (b) Saturn
(c) Mars (d) Neptune

7. 

In the given image, a cluster of star has been given. Identify the name of this specific cluster of stars.

(a) Orian (b) Ursa Major
(c) Hydra (d) Ursa Minor

8. Which of the following is the coldest planet of our Solar System?

(a) Uranus (b) Neptune
(c) Mars (d) Saturn

9. Where is the Thar Desert, one of the largest desert of the world, located?

(a) Maharashtra (b) Andhra Pradesh
(c) Bihar (d) Rajasthan

10. Which of the following is/are the means of mass communication?

(a) Radio (b) Newspaper
(c) Magazines (d) All of these

11. Who among the following proved that the Earth had no edges?

(a) Columbus (b) Ferdinand Magellan
(c) Aristotle (d) Aryabhatta

12. Which of the following cannot be considered as private transport?

(a) Trucks (b) Trains
(c) Car (d) Cycle

13. Identify the direction which shown on the top side of map.

(a) South (b) East
(c) North (d) West

14.

The image given above represents the paintings of early man. Such paintings were made by them on ....

(a) caves (b) wood (c) iron sheets (d) canvas

15. The early humans were scared from...... .

(a) fire (b) fellow humans

(c) dead animals (d) lightening and thunder

16. Identify the name of the fastest means of transport.

(a) Aeroplane (b) Railway

(c) Buses (d) Seaplane

17.

The object given in the above image was used by early men to carry the load across the river. Identify this object.

(a) Sledge (b) Cart (c) Raft (d) Logs

18. In stone age, early men used to live near which of the following river valleys of India?

(a) Ganga (b) Krishna (c) Narmada (d) Upper son

19. Which Indian festival of Muslims is celebrated after a long fast for a month?

(a) Eid (b) Muharram

(c) Ramzan (d) Easter

20. Shovana Narayan is associated with which among the following classical dance forms of India?

(a) Bharatnatyam (b) Kathakali

(c) Bihu (d) Kathak

21. Beautiful tableaux from different states and departments of governments are the major attractions in this national festival Identify the festival.

(a) Independence Day (b) Gandhi Jayanti

(c) Republic Day (d) None of these

22. Maharashtra is the main centre of which of the following industries?

(a) Jute (b) Transport

(c) Cotton textiles (d) Both (b) and (c)

23.

The image given above is related to one of the most important festival of India, in which Lord Ganesha is worshipped. This festival is generally celebrated in which of the following Indian states?

(a) Gujarat (b) Jharkhand

(c) Kerala (d) Maharashtra

24. Which of the following is/are the harvesting festival(s) of India?

(a) Pongal (b) Bihu

(c) Onam (d) All of these

25. Who composed the National Song of India, Vande Mataram?

(a) Rabindranath Tagore (b) Bankim Chandra Chatterjee

(c) Abanindranath Tagore (d) Sardar Vallabhbhai Patel

26. **Who among the following designed the Indian Rupee as the national currency of India?**

(a) Dharmalingam Udaya Kumar (b) P Chidambaran

(c) Raghu Ram Rajan (d) Rakesh Kumar Roshan

27. **Which of the following is/are the Northern states of India?**

(a) Punjab

(b) Himachal Pradesh

(c) Rajasthan

(d) All of the above

28. **Which of the following is the neighbouring state of Delhi?**

(a) Punjab (b) Rajasthan

(c) Uttar Pradesh (d) Himachal Pradesh

29. **Identify the famous sweet of Kolkata from the given options.**

(a) Chumchum (b) Sandesh

(c) Rasogulla (d) All of these

30. **Which of the following state doesn't lie in the Eastern portion of India?**

(a) Nagaland (b) Tripura

(c) Jharkhand (d) Gujarat

31. **Identify the incorrectly matched pair.**

(a) Basant Panchami – Marks the beginning of spring

(b) Independence Day – Indian flag is hoisted by President of India in Red Fort

(c) Guru Purab – Langars are organised

(d) Onam – Boat races are organised

32. **Read the given statements and select which ones are true (T) and which ones are false (F).**

I. The capital of Andhra Pradesh is Hyderabad.

II. Goa lies in the Western portion of India.

Codes

	I	II		I	II
(a)	F	T	(b)	T	T
(c)	F	F	(d)	T	F

33. Which of the following statements is incorrect?

(a) A globe shows all the places located on the Earth in detail.

(b) A map is the drawing of the Earth or a part of it on a flat surface.

(c) A compass looks like a watch and is generally used in acknowledging the directions.

(d) None of the above

34. Choose the incorrect statement.

(a) Early humans ate the shoots of plants.

(b) Early humans made tools from wood.

(c) Early humans learnt to use animal skin, leaves and barks of trees as clothing.

(d) None of the above

35. Match the following.

List I	List II
A. Postmaster	1. School
B. Surgeon	2. Post office
C. Counselor	3. Hotels
D. Chefs	4. Hospital

Codes

	A	B	C	D		A	B	C	D
(a)	3	4	1	2	(b)	1	2	3	4
(c)	2	1	4	3	(d)	2	4	1	3

Darken your choice with HB Pencil

1.	ⓐ ⓑ ⓒ ⓓ	7.	ⓐ ⓑ ⓒ ⓓ	13.	ⓐ ⓑ ⓒ ⓓ	19.	ⓐ ⓑ ⓒ ⓓ	25.	ⓐ ⓑ ⓒ ⓓ	31.	ⓐ ⓑ ⓒ ⓓ
2.	ⓐ ⓑ ⓒ ⓓ	8.	ⓐ ⓑ ⓒ ⓓ	14.	ⓐ ⓑ ⓒ ⓓ	20.	ⓐ ⓑ ⓒ ⓓ	26.	ⓐ ⓑ ⓒ ⓓ	32.	ⓐ ⓑ ⓒ ⓓ
3.	ⓐ ⓑ ⓒ ⓓ	9.	ⓐ ⓑ ⓒ ⓓ	15.	ⓐ ⓑ ⓒ ⓓ	21.	ⓐ ⓑ ⓒ ⓓ	27.	ⓐ ⓑ ⓒ ⓓ	33.	ⓐ ⓑ ⓒ ⓓ
4.	ⓐ ⓑ ⓒ ⓓ	10.	ⓐ ⓑ ⓒ ⓓ	16.	ⓐ ⓑ ⓒ ⓓ	22.	ⓐ ⓑ ⓒ ⓓ	28.	ⓐ ⓑ ⓒ ⓓ	34.	ⓐ ⓑ ⓒ ⓓ
5.	ⓐ ⓑ ⓒ ⓓ	11.	ⓐ ⓑ ⓒ ⓓ	17.	ⓐ ⓑ ⓒ ⓓ	23.	ⓐ ⓑ ⓒ ⓓ	29.	ⓐ ⓑ ⓒ ⓓ	35.	ⓐ ⓑ ⓒ ⓓ
6.	ⓐ ⓑ ⓒ ⓓ	12.	ⓐ ⓑ ⓒ ⓓ	18.	ⓐ ⓑ ⓒ ⓓ	24.	ⓐ ⓑ ⓒ ⓓ	30.	ⓐ ⓑ ⓒ ⓓ		

Answer Sheet

Chapter 01

1. (a)	**2.** (b)	**3.** (c)	**4.** (a)	**5.** (d)	**6.** (a)	**7.** (a)	**8.** (b)	**9.** (c)	**10.** (b)
11. (a)	**12.** (c)	**13.** (a)	**14.** (b)	**15.** (b)	**16.** (a)	**17.** (b)	**18.** (c)	**19.** (b)	**20.** (c)
21. (c)	**22.** (a)	**23.** (d)	**24.** (c)	**25.** (a)	**26.** (a)	**27.** (d)			

Chapter 02

1. (b)	**2.** (a)	**3.** (d)	**4.** (a)	**5.** (a)	**6.** (c)	**7.** (c)	**8.** (d)	**9.** (a)	**10.** (a)
11. (c)	**12.** (c)	**13.** (a)	**14.** (c)	**15.** (c)	**16.** (a)	**17.** (c)	**18.** (b)	**19.** (d)	**20.** (a)
21. (b)	**22.** (c)	**23.** (b)							

Chapter 03

1. (a)	**2.** (d)	**3.** (b)	**4.** (b)	**5.** (d)	**6.** (b)	**7.** (a)	**8.** (d)	**9.** (a)	**10.** (b)
11. (b)	**12.** (b)	**13.** (b)	**14.** (d)	**15.** (d)	**16.** (d)	**17.** (c)	**18.** (c)	**19.** (a)	**20.** (a)
21. (a)	**22.** (c)	**23.** (b)	**24.** (a)	**25.** (a)	**26.** (d)				

Chapter 04

1. (d)	**2.** (c)	**3.** (d)	**4.** (d)	**5.** (d)	**6.** (d)	**7.** (a)	**8.** (b)	**9.** (a)	**10.** (d)
11. (d)	**12.** (c)	**13.** (b)	**14.** (b)	**15.** (b)	**16.** (b)	**17.** (a)	**18.** (a)	**19.** (c)	**20.** (c)
21. (b)	**22.** (b)								

Chapter 05

1. (a)	**2.** (b)	**3.** (d)	**4.** (b)	**5.** (b)	**6.** (a)	**7.** (c)	**8.** (c)	**9.** (a)	**10.** (c)
11. (c)	**12.** (c)	**13.** (d)	**14.** (a)	**15.** (d)	**16.** (a)	**17.** (c)	**18.** (a)	**19.** (b)	**20.** (c)
21. (a)	**22.** (a)								

Chapter 06

1. (d)	**2.** (d)	**3.** (a)	**4.** (d)	**5.** (a)	**6.** (a)	**7.** (a)	**8.** (b)	**9.** (b)	**10.** (b)
11. (a)	**12.** (a)	**13.** (c)	**14.** (c)	**15.** (d)	**16.** (d)	**17.** (a)	**18.** (c)	**19.** (c)	**20.** (a)
21. (c)	**22.** (b)	**23.** (c)	**24.** (b)	**25.** (c)	**26.** (b)	**27.** (c)			

Chapter 07

1. (a)	**2.** (b)	**3.** (c)	**4.** (c)	**5.** (d)	**6.** (b)	**7.** (a)	**8.** (d)	**9.** (d)	**10.** (c)
11. (d)	**12.** (d)	**13.** (c)	**14.** (d)	**15.** (b)	**16.** (c)	**17.** (a)	**18.** (b)	**19.** (c)	**20.** (b)
21. (a)	**22.** (b)	**23.** (d)	**24.** (d)	**25.** (a)	**26.** (b)	**27.** (c)			

Chapter 08

1. (b)	**2.** (d)	**3.** (d)	**4.** (a)	**5.** (b)	**6.** (c)	**7.** (b)	**8.** (a)	**9.** (d)	**10.** (b)
11. (a)	**12.** (d)	**13.** (d)	**14.** (d)	**15.** (b)	**16.** (c)	**17.** (a)	**18.** (d)	**19.** (c)	**20.** (a)
21. (a)	**22.** (b)								

Chapter 09

1. (a)	**2.** (b)	**3.** (c)	**4.** (b)	**5.** (a)	**6.** (c)	**7.** (b)	**8.** (c)	**9.** (c)	**10.** (b)
11. (d)	**12.** (b)	**13.** (a)	**14.** (c)	**15.** (c)	**16.** (b)	**17.** (a)	**18.** (c)	**19.** (c)	**20.** (b)
21. (d)	**22.** (b)	**23.** (c)	**24.** (b)						

Chapter 10

1. (c)	**2.** (d)	**3.** (b)	**4.** (d)	**5.** (d)	**6.** (a)	**7.** (c)	**8.** (b)	**9.** (b)	**10.** (b)
11. (d)	**12.** (a)	**13.** (d)	**14.** (c)	**15.** (d)	**16.** (d)	**17.** (c)	**18.** (b)	**19.** (d)	**20.** (c)
21. (c)	**22.** (c)	**23.** (c)	**24.** (c)						

Practice Set 01

1. (d)	**2.** (d)	**3.** (b)	**4.** (b)	**5.** (b)	**6.** (b)	**7.** (a)	**8.** (d)	**9.** (c)	**10.** (b)
11. (b)	**12.** (c)	**13.** (a)	**14.** (d)	**15.** (c)	**16.** (d)	**17.** (b)	**18.** (c)	**19.** (a)	**20.** (b)
21. (d)	**22.** (d)	**23.** (c)	**24.** (a)	**25.** (b)	**26.** (c)	**27.** (a)	**28.** (b)	**29.** (c)	**30.** (c)
31. (a)	**32.** (d)	**33.** (c)	**34.** (c)	**35.** (a)					

Practice Set 02

1. (c)	**2.** (d)	**3.** (b)	**4.** (d)	**5.** (b)	**6.** (d)	**7.** (b)	**8.** (a)	**9.** (d)	**10.** (d)
11. (b)	**12.** (b)	**13.** (c)	**14.** (a)	**15.** (d)	**16.** (a)	**17.** (c)	**18.** (d)	**19.** (a)	**20.** (d)
21. (c)	**22.** (c)	**23.** (d)	**24.** (d)	**25.** (b)	**26.** (a)	**27.** (d)	**28.** (c)	**29.** (d)	**30.** (d)
31. (b)	**32.** (a)	**33.** (d)	**34.** (d)	**35.** (d)					